Women of the Bible

By Karajah Yashar

BLACKSTONE PUBLISHING

Orlando, FL

Women of the Bible

www.BSPBooks.com

Developed by Karajah Yashar

ISBN: 978-1-962691-22-2

First Edition: June 2024

Table of Contents

Introduction

The role of women in the Bible is one of significant importance, often underestimated or overlooked in traditional interpretations. Throughout the scriptures, women play diverse and crucial roles that contribute to the unfolding narrative of God's redemptive plan for humanity. From the Old Testament to the New Testament, women are depicted as leaders, prophets, disciples, mothers, and faithful followers of God, whose actions and contributions shape the course of history and reveal profound truths about faith, resilience, and the character of God.

One of the most notable examples of women's importance in the Bible is found in the Old Testament book of Genesis with the story of Eve, the first woman created by God. While often associated with the Fall, Eve's role extends beyond this singular event. She is portrayed as a partner to Adam, sharing in the responsibility of stewardship over creation. Additionally, Eve's descendants, including Sarah, Rebekah, Rachel, and Leah, are central figures in the lineage of the Israelite patriarchs, demonstrating their vital role in the continuation of God's covenant promises.

In the narratives of the Old Testament, we encounter numerous women who defy societal norms and expectations to fulfill God's purposes. Women like Deborah, the prophetess and judge of Israel, and Esther, the queen who risks her life to save her people, exemplify courage, wisdom, and faithfulness in the face of adversity. These women challenge traditional gender roles and demonstrate that God's call and empowerment are not limited by gender.

Moreover, the New Testament presents a revolutionary perspective on the role of women in the life and ministry of Jesus Christ. Jesus' interactions with women, including Mary Magdalene, the Samaritan woman at the well, and the woman with the issue of blood, reveal his radical inclusion and affirmation of women as equal recipients of God's grace and salvation. Jesus' teachings and actions affirm the dignity, worth, and value of women in a society where they were often marginalized and oppressed.

Furthermore, women play a pivotal role in the early Christian church, serving as leaders, teachers, and evangelists. The apostle Paul acknowledges the contributions of women like Phoebe, Junia, and Priscilla in his letters, affirming their partnership in the spread of the gospel. Despite cultural barriers and societal constraints, women in the early church actively participated in ministry and played integral roles in the expansion of God's kingdom.

In conclusion, the Bible portrays women as central figures in the unfolding narrative of God's redemptive plan for humanity. Their stories serve as powerful reminders of God's inclusive love and affirmation of all people, regardless of gender. Women in the Bible challenge traditional stereotypes and expectations, demonstrating courage, faithfulness, and leadership in the face of adversity. Their contributions enrich the biblical narrative and inspire believers to recognize and affirm the inherent dignity and worth of women in all areas of life and ministry.

The Virtuous Woman

The virtuous woman or the woman of noble character, is portrayed in the final chapter of the book of Proverbs in the Bible. This passage, consisting of verses 10-31, presents a vivid description of a woman who exemplifies wisdom, strength, diligence, and virtue in all aspects of her life. The Proverbs 31 woman serves as a timeless model of godly womanhood, offering valuable insights and principles for women of all ages and backgrounds.

The passage begins by praising the virtuous woman's worth, describing her as more precious than rubies and far surpassing the value of material wealth. She is depicted as a woman of integrity and honor, whose character is marked by wisdom, kindness, and strength. Throughout the passage, various aspects of her life are highlighted, showcasing her multifaceted roles and responsibilities.

One of the defining characteristics of the Proverbs 31 woman is her industriousness and diligence in her work. She is described as a capable and resourceful manager of her household, overseeing the well-being of her family and servants with wisdom and efficiency. She rises early to provide food for her household and tends to her duties with vigor and purpose. Her industriousness extends beyond the home as she engages in commerce, buying and selling goods to provide for her family's needs and contribute to their financial security.

Additionally, the Proverbs 31 woman is praised for her strength and resilience in the face of challenges. She is depicted as a woman of noble character who faces adversity with confidence and courage. Her strength comes not only from physical prowess but also from her unwavering faith in God and her commitment to fulfilling her responsibilities with excellence.

Furthermore, the Proverbs 31 woman is characterized by her compassion and generosity towards others. She extends her hand to the poor and needy, demonstrating a heart of compassion and a willingness to use her resources to help those in need. Her kindness and generosity are a reflection of her commitment to living a life of service and love towards others.

Ultimately, the Proverbs 31 woman's greatest strength lies in her fear of the Lord. She is described as a woman who reverences God and seeks to live according to His commands. Her wisdom, strength, and virtue flow from her relationship with God, as she trusts in His guidance and seeks to honor Him in all that she does.

In conclusion, the Proverbs 31 woman stands as a timeless example of godly womanhood, embodying qualities of wisdom, strength, diligence, and virtue. Her life serves as a model for women of all generations, offering valuable insights and principles for living a life of purpose, integrity, and godliness. By emulating the virtues of the Proverbs

31 woman, women can cultivate lives that honor God, bless others, and bring glory to His name.

Eve

Eve, the first woman created by God according to the book of Genesis in the Bible, occupies a significant and complex role in the narrative of humanity's origins. Her story, depicted in Genesis chapters 2 and 3, serves as a foundational account that explores themes of creation, temptation, and the consequences of disobedience. While Eve is often associated with the Fall of humanity, her character and actions offer valuable insights into the complexities of human nature and the redemptive plan of God.

Eve's creation is described in Genesis 2:21-22, where God forms her from Adam's rib, signifying her equality and partnership with him. As Adam's companion, Eve shares in the responsibility of stewardship over the Garden of Eden and participates in the intimate relationship with God. She is portrayed as Adam's counterpart, completing him in a profound and meaningful way.

However, Eve's role in the narrative takes a dramatic turn with the introduction of the serpent and the temptation to eat from the forbidden tree of the knowledge of good and evil. In Genesis 3:6, Eve succumbs to the serpent's deception and partakes of the fruit, leading to the disobedience that results in humanity's expulsion from paradise. While Eve's decision is often viewed negatively, her motivations and intentions are subject to interpretation. Some interpretations suggest that Eve's desire for knowledge and autonomy led her to disobey God's command, while others emphasize the subtlety of the serpent's deception and Eve's vulnerability to temptation.

Despite the consequences of her actions, Eve's story is not defined solely by her fall from grace. She is also depicted as the mother of all living beings, symbolizing the beginning of human civilization and the continuation of God's covenant promises. Eve's descendants, including Cain, Abel, and Seth, play significant roles in the unfolding narrative of salvation history, demonstrating God's ability to work through flawed and imperfect individuals to accomplish His purposes.

Moreover, Eve's story offers valuable lessons about the complexities of human nature and the reality of sin and its consequences. Her experience serves as a cautionary tale about the dangers of disobedience and the importance of trusting in God's wisdom and guidance. Additionally, Eve's story highlights the significance of redemption and restoration, as God promises to send a Savior who will ultimately triumph over sin and death.

Eve's role in the Bible is multifaceted and complex, encompassing both her fall from grace and her significance as the mother of all humanity. While her actions have far-reaching consequences, Eve's story also reflects themes of redemption, hope, and the enduring faithfulness of God. By examining Eve's story, readers are invited to reflect on the complexities of human nature, the reality of sin, and the transformative power of God's grace and mercy.

Sarah

Sarah, the wife of Abraham, is a prominent figure in the Bible, particularly in the book of Genesis. Her story, spanning several chapters, offers valuable insights into faith, patience, and the sovereignty of God. Despite facing numerous trials and challenges, Sarah's life serves as a testament to

God's faithfulness and His ability to fulfill His promises in unexpected ways.

Sarah's story begins in Genesis 11, where she is introduced as Abram's wife. The couple, who are childless and advanced in years, are called by God to leave their homeland and journey to a land that God will show them. This call sets in motion a series of events that will ultimately shape the course of biblical history.

One of the central themes of Sarah's story is the struggle with infertility and the longing for a child. Despite God's promise to make Abram's descendants as numerous as the stars in the sky, Sarah remains barren for many years. In her desperation, Sarah gives her maidservant, Hagar, to Abram as a surrogate mother, resulting in the birth of Ishmael. This decision, borne out of impatience and doubt, creates tension and conflict within the family and has far-reaching consequences.

However, Sarah's faith is ultimately vindicated when, at the age of ninety, she miraculously conceives and gives birth to Isaac, the child of promise. This miraculous birth not only fulfills God's covenant with Abram but also serves as a testament to God's power to bring life out of barrenness and to fulfill His promises in His timing. Sarah's joy at Isaac's birth is evident, and she declares, "God has brought me laughter, and everyone who hears about this will laugh with me" (Genesis 21:6).

Sarah's story also highlights her role as a matriarch and leader within her family. Despite the patriarchal nature of ancient society, Sarah exercises authority and influence, particularly in matters concerning her son Isaac and his inheritance. She is portrayed as a woman of strength, intelligence, and resourcefulness, who plays a pivotal role in shaping the destiny of her family and descendants.

Furthermore, Sarah's story serves as a reminder of the importance of faith and trust in God's promises, even in the face of seemingly insurmountable obstacles. Despite her initial doubts and moments of weakness, Sarah ultimately comes to trust in God's faithfulness and His ability to fulfill His promises in His timing and His way.

Sarah's story is one of faith, perseverance, and the fulfillment of God's promises. Her journey from barrenness to motherhood serves as a powerful testament to God's faithfulness and His ability to bring life out of barrenness. Through Sarah's story, readers are reminded of the importance of trusting in God's timing, even when circumstances seem bleak, and of the power of faith to overcome obstacles and bring about His purposes.

Rebekah

Rebekah, a central figure in the book of Genesis, plays a significant role in the narrative of the patriarchs and matriarchs of Israel. Her story, which spans several chapters in Genesis, offers valuable insights into faith, providence, and the complexities of human relationships. Rebekah's life serves as a testament to God's sovereignty and His ability to work through imperfect individuals to accomplish His purposes.

Rebekah's story begins in Genesis 24, where she is introduced as the young maiden chosen by God to become the wife of Isaac, the son of Abraham. Abraham sends his servant to find a suitable wife for Isaac from among his relatives, and God leads the servant to Rebekah, who demonstrates kindness, hospitality, and humility by offering water to him and his camels. This encounter serves as a divine confirmation of God's choice, and Rebekah agrees to accompany the servant back to Isaac.

Upon meeting Isaac, Rebekah becomes his wife, and their marriage is marked by love, devotion, and mutual respect. Despite facing challenges and trials, including barrenness, Rebekah remains faithful to Isaac and supports him in his role as the patriarch of their family.

One of the most significant events in Rebekah's life occurs with the birth of her twin sons, Jacob and Esau. Rebekah's pregnancy is fraught with conflict, as the twins struggle within her womb, foreshadowing the rivalry and tension that will characterize their relationship. Rebekah receives a divine revelation that the older son, Esau, will serve the younger son, Jacob, indicating God's sovereign choice of Jacob to inherit the blessing of the covenant.

Rebekah's actions surrounding the blessing of Jacob further demonstrate her resourcefulness and determination to fulfill God's plan. She devises a plan to deceive Isaac into bestowing the blessing upon Jacob instead of Esau, disguising Jacob with goat skins to resemble his hairy brother. Although Rebekah's methods may be controversial, her actions align with God's divine purposes and contribute to the fulfillment of His covenant with Abraham.

Despite her flaws and shortcomings, Rebekah's story exemplifies the theme of God's providential care and guidance throughout her life. Her journey from a young maiden to the matriarch of a great nation is marked by moments of faith, courage, and obedience to God's leading. Rebekah's role in shaping the destiny of her family and descendants underscores the importance of individual agency and the sovereign hand of God working in tandem to fulfill His purposes.

Rebekah's tale unfolds as a captivating saga of faith, divine intervention, and the intricate dynamics of human connections. Her journey stands as a powerful testament to the sovereignty of God, showcasing His remarkable ability to use flawed individuals to fulfill His divine plans. Through Rebekah's narrative, readers are prompted to embrace the profound lesson of placing unwavering trust in God's direction and faithfully following His path, even amidst life's uncertainties and challenges.

Leah

Leah, the elder daughter of Laban and the first wife of Jacob, is a compelling figure in the biblical narrative, particularly in the book of Genesis. Despite initially being overshadowed by her sister Rachel, Leah's story is one of resilience, faith, and unexpected blessings. Her journey, marked by personal struggles and triumphs, offers valuable insights into themes of identity, acceptance, and the sovereignty of God.

Leah's story begins in Genesis 29, where she is introduced as the elder daughter of Laban and is given in marriage to Jacob through a deceptive act orchestrated by her father. Unlike her younger sister Rachel, who is described as beautiful and favored by Jacob, Leah is described as having "weak eyes." This description likely implies that Leah was not as physically attractive as Rachel, which may have contributed to her feelings of insecurity and inadequacy.

Despite her initial disadvantages, Leah's story takes a surprising turn when she becomes the mother of Jacob's first four sons: Reuben, Simeon, Levi, and Judah. Each of these births is accompanied by expressions of hope and gratitude from Leah, who sees her sons as evidence of God's favor and blessing. In naming her sons, Leah expresses her longing for acceptance and affection from her husband, hoping that each child will bring her closer to Jacob's heart.

Leah's relationship with Rachel is characterized by rivalry and competition, as they vie for Jacob's love and attention. However, their rivalry also serves as a catalyst for personal growth and transformation.

Despite their differences, Leah and Rachel ultimately share a deep bond as sisters, supporting each other through the joys and sorrows of life.

One of the most poignant moments in Leah's story occurs when she acknowledges her dependence on God for validation and acceptance. After giving birth to her fourth son, Judah, Leah declares, "This time I will praise the Lord," expressing her gratitude for God's faithfulness and provision in her life. This moment of surrender and gratitude marks a turning point in Leah's journey, as she comes to recognize her worth and identity as a beloved child of God, regardless of her outward appearance or the opinions of others.

Leah's narrative defies conventional standards of beauty and value, weaving a profound tale that echoes the timeless truth: true worth transcends mere appearances, resonating in the embrace and devotion of God. Amidst the harsh sting of rejection and societal dismissal, Leah unearths her intrinsic worth and calling within the unwavering affection and faithfulness of her Creator. Her journey stands as a resounding testament to the profound truth that God's unwavering gaze perceives and treasures every soul for their essence, illuminating His intricate plans designed for their flourishing and fulfillment.

Leah's story is one of transformation, redemption, and the unexpected blessings that come from trusting in God's providence. Through her journey, readers are encouraged to embrace their identity as beloved children of God and to find their worth and significance in His unfailing love. Like Leah, believers are challenged to trust in God's faithfulness, knowing that He is always at work, bringing beauty out of brokenness and joy out of sorrow.

Rachel

Rachel's story, which unfolds in Genesis chapters 29-35, is characterized by themes of love, rivalry, faith, and redemption. Rachel's life serves as a poignant reminder of the complexities of human relationships and the enduring faithfulness of God in the midst of adversity.

Rachel is introduced in Genesis 29 as the younger daughter of Laban, the brother of Rebekah, and the beloved wife of Jacob. From the moment Jacob sets eyes on Rachel at the well, he is captivated by her beauty and charm, and he makes a covenant with Laban to work for seven years in exchange for Rachel's hand in marriage. However, Laban deceives Jacob by giving him Leah, Rachel's older sister, in marriage instead. Jacob agrees to work another seven years for Rachel, demonstrating the depth of his love and devotion to her.

Despite being Jacob's favored wife, Rachel's life is marked by hardship and struggle. She faces the pain of infertility, watching as her sister Leah bears son after son while she remains barren. Rachel's longing for children is palpable, and she cries out to God in anguish, pleading for His intervention. Her prayers are eventually answered when God remembers Rachel and opens her womb, blessing her with a son named Joseph, whom she describes as a "child of my sorrow" but also a source of great joy and hope.

Rachel's relationship with her sister Leah is complex and fraught with tension, as they vie for Jacob's affection and attention. Despite their rivalry, Rachel and Leah share a deep bond as sisters, and they support each other through the challenges they face as wives and mothers.

Tragically, Rachel's life is cut short during the birth of her second son, Benjamin, as she dies in childbirth and is buried along the road to Bethlehem. Her premature death is a poignant reminder of the fragility of life and the pain of loss, but it also serves as a testament to her enduring legacy as the mother of two of the twelve tribes of Israel.

Despite the trials and tribulations she faces, Rachel's story is ultimately one of faith and redemption. Her unwavering love for Jacob, her fervent prayers for children, and her enduring hope in God's promises demonstrate her deep faith and trust in God's faithfulness. Through Rachel's life, readers are reminded of the importance of trusting in God's timing and His ability to bring beauty out of brokenness, joy out of sorrow, and hope out of despair.

Rachel's story is a powerful reminder of the complexities of human relationships and the enduring faithfulness of God in the midst of adversity. Her life serves as a testament to the power of love, faith, and redemption to overcome even the greatest challenges. Through Rachel's story, readers are inspired to trust in God's promises, to persevere in the face of trials, and to find hope and healing in His unfailing love.

Jochebed

Jochebed, the mother of Moses, stands as a remarkable figure in the biblical narrative, celebrated for her courage, faith, and maternal love. Despite living in a time of oppression and persecution, Jochebed's unwavering trust in God and her sacrificial actions play a pivotal role in the deliverance of the Israelites from slavery in Egypt.

Her story, found primarily in the book of Exodus, serves as a powerful testament to the resilience of the human spirit and the providential care of God in the face of adversity.

Jochebed's story begins in Exodus 2, during a time when the Israelites are suffering under the oppressive rule of Pharaoh in Egypt. In the midst of this harsh reality, Jochebed gives birth to a son, whom she hides for three months to protect him from Pharaoh's decree to kill all Hebrew male infants. When she can no longer conceal him, Jochebed places her baby in a basket and sets him adrift on the Nile River, entrusting his fate to God's care.

Despite the inherent risks and uncertainties of her actions, Jochebed's decision to place her son in the Nile is an act of profound faith and courage. Rather than succumb to fear or despair, she demonstrates her trust in God's sovereignty and His ability to protect and preserve her child. Her actions reflect a deep-seated belief in God's faithfulness to His promises and His power to bring about deliverance in the most unlikely of circumstances.

Miraculously, Jochebed's son is discovered by Pharaoh's daughter while she is bathing in the river, and she takes pity on the child and decides to raise him as her own. Through a series of providential events, Jochebed is reunited with her son, whom she names Moses, meaning "drawn out," symbolizing the miraculous circumstances of his birth and rescue.

Jochebed's role in Moses' life extends beyond his infancy, as she continues to play a formative role in shaping his character and faith. Despite entrusting him to the care of Pharaoh's daughter, Jochebed remains connected to her son, providing him with a foundation of faith and identity rooted in his Hebrew heritage. Her influence on Moses is evident throughout his life, as he demonstrates courage, compassion, and a deep sense of justice in his leadership of the Israelites.

Jochebed's legacy as a mother of faith and courage endures throughout the biblical narrative and serves as an inspiration to believers of all generations. Her willingness to trust God in the face of adversity, her sacrificial love for her children, and her unwavering commitment to God's purposes exemplify the qualities of a godly mother and a faithful servant of God. Through Jochebed's story, readers are reminded of the power of faith, love, and obedience to overcome the greatest of challenges and to bring about God's purposes in the world.

Zipporah

Zipporah, the wife of Moses, is a significant yet often overlooked figure in the biblical narrative. Her story, found primarily in the book of Exodus, offers valuable insights into themes of faith, obedience, and cultural diversity. Despite her relatively brief appearance in the biblical text, Zipporah's actions and character reveal her strength, resourcefulness, and devotion to God and her family.

Zipporah's story begins in Exodus 2, where she is introduced as the daughter of Jethro, a priest of Midian. Moses, having fled Egypt after killing an Egyptian taskmaster, encounters Zipporah and her sisters at a well in the land of Midian. Moved by their plight, Moses defends the women from hostile shepherds and is invited to their home by Jethro, who offers him hospitality and eventually gives Zipporah to Moses in marriage.

Zipporah's marriage to Moses marks the beginning of a new chapter in her life, as she becomes the wife of the man chosen by God to lead the Israelites out of slavery in Egypt. Despite the challenges and uncertainties that lie ahead, Zipporah demonstrates her faith and commitment to Moses and his mission.

One of the most notable incidents involving Zipporah occurs in Exodus 4, when God seeks to kill Moses for neglecting to circumcise their son. In a bold and decisive act, Zipporah takes a flint knife and circumcises her son, thereby averting God's wrath and saving Moses' life. This act of obedience and courage highlights Zipporah's role as a faithful partner to Moses and her willingness to do whatever is necessary to fulfill God's commands.

Zipporah's cultural background as a Midianite also plays a significant role in her story, highlighting the diversity of God's people and the universality of His redemptive plan. Despite being a foreigner in the land of Israel, Zipporah is embraced as a member of God's covenant community through her marriage to Moses and her participation in the events of Israel's deliverance from Egypt.

While Zipporah's appearances in the biblical narrative are relatively brief, her character and actions leave a lasting impression. Her faith, obedience, and cultural diversity serve as a reminder of God's faithfulness to all people, regardless of their background or nationality. Through Zipporah's story, readers are reminded of the importance of faithfulness, courage, and obedience in fulfilling God's purposes, as well as the richness and diversity of God's people throughout history.

Zipporah's narrative within the Bible weaves a compelling tapestry of faith, bravery, and cultural richness. As Moses' devoted wife and a vital participant in God's redemptive narrative, Zipporah's resolute actions and unwavering character resonate with an enduring legacy of fidelity and commitment. Her tale beckons readers to embrace the expansive and inclusive community of God, illustrating that His boundless love and redemption extend to all who place their trust in Him.

Miriam

Miriam, the sister of Moses and Aaron, has an important role for the Hebrew Nation, particularly in the Exodus account of the Israelites' deliverance from slavery in Egypt. Her story, found primarily in the books of Exodus, Numbers, and Micah, highlights her role as a prophetess, leader, and worshipper, whose faith and courage contribute to the fulfillment of God's purposes for His people.

Miriam's story begins in Exodus 2, where she plays a crucial role in the preservation of her brother Moses' life. When Pharaoh decrees that all Hebrew male infants must be killed, Miriam, along with her mother Jochebed, places Moses in a basket and sets him adrift on the Nile River. Miriam watches over her brother from a distance, ensuring his safety and eventual rescue by Pharaoh's daughter. Through this act of courage and faith, Miriam demonstrates her deep love for her brother and her commitment to God's plan for His people.

As Moses grows into adulthood and emerges as the leader of the Israelites, Miriam's influence and leadership become more pronounced. In Exodus 15, following the miraculous crossing of the Red Sea, Miriam leads the women of Israel in a song of praise and thanksgiving to God. Her role as a worship leader highlights her spiritual insight and her ability to inspire others to praise and worship God in times of triumph and adversity.

Miriam's status as a prophetess is further emphasized in Numbers 12, where she, along with Aaron, challenges Moses' leadership and authority. Despite being rebuked by God for their rebellion,

Miriam's prophetic gift is affirmed, as God speaks to Aaron and Miriam directly, declaring, "When there is a prophet among you, I, the Lord, reveal myself to them in visions, I speak to them in dreams" (Numbers 12:6). Miriam's role as a prophetess underscores her intimate relationship with God and her unique calling to speak His word to His people.

Although Miriam's life is not without its challenges and failures, including her rebellion against Moses and her subsequent punishment with leprosy, her legacy as a faithful servant of God endures. Her leadership, courage, and devotion to God's purposes serve as an inspiration to believers of all generations, reminding them of the importance of faith, obedience, and humility in serving God and His people.

Miriam's narrative epitomizes a journey of profound faith, unyielding courage, and visionary leadership, marked by her steadfast dedication to God's unfolding plan for His people. As a revered prophetess, revered worship leader, and beloved sister to Moses, Miriam's sphere of influence extends far beyond her familial ties, shaping the destiny of the entire nation of Israel. Her enduring legacy serves as a compelling call to believers, urging them to embrace their divine calling, entrust themselves to God's unwavering faithfulness, and serve Him with unwavering humility and unwavering devotion, reassured by the unshakeable truth that He faithfully fulfills His every promise.

Rahab

Rahab, a woman of Jericho, is a captivating figure in the Old Testament, celebrated for her courage, faith, and unexpected role in the story of Israel's conquest of Canaan. Her narrative, found primarily in the book of Joshua, offers profound insights into themes of redemption, inclusion, and the transformative power of faith. Despite her marginalized status as a Canaanite prostitute, Rahab's remarkable act of hospitality and her subsequent inclusion in the lineage of Jesus Christ elevate her to a position of honor and significance in biblical history.

Rahab's introduction in the biblical narrative occurs during Joshua's reconnaissance mission to the city of Jericho in preparation for the Israelite invasion. As a prostitute, Rahab resides in a house built into the city wall, making her an unlikely candidate for heroism and redemption. However, when Joshua's spies seek refuge in her home, Rahab demonstrates extraordinary courage and faith by hiding them from the city authorities and providing them with crucial intelligence about Jericho's defenses.

Rahab's decision to shelter the Israelite spies is motivated by her recognition of the power and sovereignty of their God. She confesses to the spies, "I know that the Lord has given you the land, and that the fear of you has fallen upon us, and that all the inhabitants of the land melt away before you" (Joshua 2:9). Rahab's acknowledgment of God's supremacy and her plea for mercy demonstrate her faith and humility, paving the way for her salvation and the salvation of her family.

As a reward for her faithfulness and hospitality, the Israelite spies spare Rahab and her household from the destruction of Jericho when the city falls to the Israelite army. Rahab and her family are incorporated into the community of Israel, where they dwell among the people of God and eventually become ancestors of King David and, ultimately, Jesus Christ Himself.

Rahab's inclusion in the lineage of Jesus Christ is a remarkable testament to the transformative power of faith and the universality of God's redemptive plan. Despite her background and social status, Rahab's courageous act of faith secures her a place of honor in the annals of biblical history, demonstrating that God's grace extends to all who place their trust in Him.

Moreover, Rahab's story challenges conventional notions of righteousness and religious exclusivity. As a Canaanite woman, Rahab occupies a marginalized position in Israelite society, yet her faith and actions earn her a place among God's chosen people. Her inclusion in the lineage of Jesus Christ serves as a powerful reminder that God's love knows no bounds and that salvation is available to all who call upon His name in faith.

Rahab's biblical tale unfolds as a riveting narrative of extraordinary courage, unwavering faith, and profound redemption. Despite her humble beginnings and marginalized societal status, Rahab's bold act of hospitality and steadfast trust in God elevate her to a place of honor within the lineage of Jesus Christ. Her compelling example challenges readers to confront their own biases and prejudices, compelling them to acknowledge the transformative influence of faith in God's redemptive design. Rahab's story resonates as a timeless testament to the expansive reach of God's grace, embracing all who earnestly seek Him in faith, transcending barriers of background or social standing.

Naomi

Naomi, a central figure in the book of Ruth, stands as a poignant example of resilience, faith, and the redemptive power of God's providence. Her story, found in the Old Testament, offers valuable insights into themes of loss, loyalty, and restoration, as well as the enduring bond of family and the steadfastness of God's love.

Naomi's story begins in the land of Bethlehem during a time of famine. Along with her husband Elimelech and their two sons, Mahlon and Chilion, Naomi migrates to the land of Moab in search of sustenance and security. However, tragedy strikes when Naomi's husband dies, leaving her a widow in a foreign land. Despite her grief and uncertainty, Naomi remains steadfast in her faith and devotion to God.

Naomi's sorrow deepens with the deaths of her two sons, leaving her bereft and destitute. Alone in a foreign land, Naomi faces the prospect of a bleak and uncertain future. Yet, even in the midst of her despair, Naomi clings to her faith in God and demonstrates remarkable strength and resilience.

Naomi's decision to return to Bethlehem, the land of her people, marks a turning point in her story. Accompanied by her daughter-in-law Ruth, who refuses to leave her side, Naomi embarks on a journey of redemption and restoration. Despite her initial reluctance to burden Ruth with the hardships that lie ahead, Naomi eventually accepts Ruth's steadfast loyalty and companionship, recognizing the depth of her daughter-in-law's commitment and love.

Upon their return to Bethlehem, Naomi's presence evokes both sympathy and curiosity among the townspeople, who marvel at her transformation and inquire about her well-being. In a poignant moment of vulnerability and honesty, Naomi responds to their inquiries by declaring, "Do not call me Naomi; call me Mara, for the Almighty has dealt very bitterly with me" (Ruth 1:20). Through these words, Naomi acknowledges the depth of her grief and despair, while also expressing her unwavering trust in God's providential care.

Naomi's story reaches its climax with the arrival of the harvest season, which brings with it the promise of provision and renewal. Through a series of providential events orchestrated by God, Naomi and Ruth are brought into the care and protection of Boaz, a wealthy landowner and relative of Naomi's deceased husband. Boaz's kindness and generosity serve as a tangible expression of God's faithfulness and provision, ultimately leading to the restoration of Naomi's family and legacy.

In the end, Naomi's story is one of hope, redemption, and the enduring faithfulness of God. Despite experiencing profound loss and hardship, Naomi remains steadfast in her trust in God's promises, ultimately experiencing the restoration and renewal of her family and legacy. Through her story, readers are reminded of the power of faith, loyalty, and perseverance in the face of adversity, as well as the transformative impact of God's providential care and love.

Naomi's biblical narrative stands as an enduring testament to the indomitable resilience of the human spirit and the transformative might of God's providential care. Amidst the trials of loss, grief, and eventual restoration, Naomi emerges as a beacon of hope and unwavering faith, her journey inspiring readers to anchor their trust in God's steadfast faithfulness and provision, even amidst life's deepest shadows. Her tale resonates across generations of believers, offering profound insights into the complexities of suffering, the vital role of community, and the unwavering constancy of God's boundless love.

Ruth

Ruth, a central figure in the Old Testament, is celebrated for her remarkable journey of loyalty, love, and redemption. Her story, chronicled in the book of Ruth, offers profound insights into themes of faithfulness, providence, and the transformative power of love. Despite facing adversity and uncertainty, Ruth's unwavering commitment to her mother-in-law Naomi and her steadfast trust in God's guidance ultimately lead to her inclusion in the lineage of King David and, ultimately, Jesus Christ.

Ruth's story begins in the land of Moab during a time of famine in Bethlehem. Following the death of her husband, Mahlon, Ruth chooses to accompany her mother-in-law Naomi back to Bethlehem, despite the challenges and uncertainties of such a journey. Ruth's decision to remain with Naomi, rather than returning to her homeland and seeking security and comfort, is a testament to her loyalty and devotion to her family.

Upon their arrival in Bethlehem, Ruth's humility and industriousness quickly earn her favor among the townspeople. Determined to provide for herself and Naomi, Ruth gleans in the fields of Boaz, a wealthy landowner and relative of Naomi's deceased husband. Boaz's kindness and generosity towards Ruth, as well as his recognition of her character and virtue, set the stage for the unfolding of God's providential plan.

One of the most poignant moments in Ruth's story occurs when she declares her commitment to Naomi in a heartfelt vow, saying, "Where you go, I will go, and where you stay, I will stay. Your people will be my people and your God my God" (Ruth 1:16). This declaration of loyalty and faithfulness reflects Ruth's deep devotion to Naomi and her willingness to embrace a new identity and allegiance in service to her mother-in-law and her God.

As the story progresses, Ruth's relationship with Boaz deepens, culminating in their marriage and the birth of their son, Obed. Through God's providential care and guidance, Ruth is blessed with a family and a legacy that extends far beyond her own lifetime. Obed, the son of Ruth and Boaz, becomes the father of Jesse, who in turn is the father of King David, the greatest king of Israel.

Ruth's inclusion in the lineage of King David and, ultimately, Jesus Christ, underscores the significance of her story in the biblical narrative. Despite her humble origins and foreign heritage, Ruth's faithfulness, courage, and love serve as a shining example of God's redemptive work in the lives of ordinary individuals. Through her story, readers are reminded of the transformative power of love, the importance of loyalty and faithfulness, and the certainty of God's providence in the midst of life's uncertainties.

Ruth's narrative within the biblical text serves as an enduring testimony to the transformative qualities of love, loyalty, and unwavering faithfulness. Her remarkable journey, from a foreign widow to a revered ancestor within the lineage of King David and ultimately Jesus Christ, stands as a profound testament to the redemptive agency inherent in God's interaction with His people. Ruth's narrative encourages readers to emulate her embodiment of devotion, courage, and steadfast trust in God's providential care, illustrating the belief that divine intervention operates ceaselessly to yield beauty from brokenness and joy from sorrow.

Bathsheba

Bathsheba, a woman whose name evokes both intrigue and tragedy, is a central figure in one of the most famous episodes of the Old Testament. Her story, found primarily in the books of 2 Samuel and 1 Kings, is marked by themes of power, betrayal, and redemption, offering profound insights into human nature and the consequences of sin.

Despite being known primarily as the object of King David's desire, Bathsheba's story transcends mere scandal, revealing her resilience and eventual role as the mother of Solomon, one of Israel's greatest kings.

Bathsheba's introduction in the biblical narrative occurs during a pivotal moment in King David's reign. While the king's army is away at war, Bathsheba is bathing on her rooftop when David, from his vantage point in the palace, sees her and is overcome with desire. Despite knowing that Bathsheba is the wife of Uriah the Hittite, one of his loyal soldiers, David summons her to the palace and commits adultery with her.

The consequences of David's actions are dire and far-reaching. Bathsheba becomes pregnant with David's child, leading the king to orchestrate a cover-up that ultimately results in the death of Uriah and a divine judgment pronounced upon David's house. Despite these tragedies, Bathsheba's story does not end in despair. After the death of her first child, she becomes the wife of David and bears him another son, Solomon, whom the Lord loves and appoints as David's successor.

Bathsheba's role as the mother of Solomon is significant, as it underscores the redemptive nature of her story. Despite the circumstances of his conception, Solomon becomes one of Israel's most beloved and wise kings, renowned for his wisdom, wealth, and accomplishments. Bathsheba's maternal influence plays a crucial role in Solomon's upbringing, shaping him into the leader he becomes.

Bathsheba's story challenges traditional interpretations that portray her solely as a victim or temptress. While she is certainly vulnerable to the abuses of power and authority, Bathsheba's resilience and eventual elevation to the status of queen mother demonstrate her agency and strength. Despite the injustices and tragedies she endures, Bathsheba emerges as a central figure in the Davidic dynasty, playing a pivotal role in the establishment of Solomon's reign and the preservation of David's legacy.

Bathsheba's narrative stands as a poignant cautionary tale, illuminating the perils of unchecked power and underscoring the vital importance of accountability and repentance. David's misuse of his kingly authority sets in motion a chain of grave consequences that reverberate through the lives of Bathsheba, himself, and their families, revealing the destructive impact of sin left unchecked.

Bathsheba's story vividly underscores the urgent need for genuine repentance and sincere efforts toward reconciliation in the face of moral transgressions.

Bathsheba's story in the Bible is a complex and multifaceted narrative that transcends mere scandal to reveal themes of power, betrayal, and redemption. Despite the tragedies and injustices she endures, Bathsheba's resilience and eventual role as the mother of Solomon underscore the redemptive nature of her story. Through her example, readers are challenged to confront the complexities of human nature and the consequences of sin, while also finding hope in the possibility of redemption and reconciliation.

Abigail

Abigail, a woman of intelligence, wisdom, and courage, is a prominent figure in the Old Testament, particularly in the book of 1 Samuel. Her story offers profound insights into themes of humility, peacemaking, and the power of a gentle and discerning spirit. Despite facing adversity and danger, Abigail's actions demonstrate her commitment to righteousness and her unwavering trust in God's providence.

Abigail's story unfolds in 1 Samuel 25, where she is introduced as the wife of Nabal, a wealthy but foolish man who behaves harshly and arrogantly towards David, the future king of Israel. When David and his men, who have been providing protection for Nabal's flocks, request provisions from him in accordance with the custom of the time, Nabal responds with ingratitude and contempt, provoking David's wrath.

Upon learning of Nabal's foolishness and the danger it poses to her family, Abigail takes decisive action to intervene and prevent disaster. Despite the risk to her own safety, Abigail gathers a generous supply of provisions and sets out to meet David and his men before they can exact vengeance on Nabal and his household.

In a moment of remarkable diplomacy and wisdom, Abigail approaches David with humility and respect, acknowledging his rightful place as the future king of Israel and appealing to his sense of justice and mercy. She offers David the provisions he requested and pleads for forgiveness on behalf of her foolish husband, recognizing the folly of his actions and seeking to avert bloodshed and tragedy.

David, deeply impressed by Abigail's wisdom and integrity, relents from his plan of vengeance and accepts her offerings. He praises Abigail for her discernment and courage, declaring, "Blessed be your discretion, and blessed be you, who have kept me this day from bloodguilt and from avenging myself with my own hand" (1 Samuel 25:33).

Abigail's intervention not only saves her household from destruction but also earns her the admiration and respect of David and his men. When Nabal dies shortly thereafter, David recognizes God's hand at work in Abigail's actions and takes her as his wife, elevating her to a position of honor and influence in his court.

Abigail's story serves as a powerful example of the transformative power of wisdom, humility, and peacemaking in the face of conflict and danger. Her actions demonstrate the importance of discernment and diplomacy in resolving disputes and fostering reconciliation, even in the most challenging circumstances.

In conclusion, Abigail's story in the Bible is a testament to the power of wisdom, humility, and courage in the face of adversity. Her intervention in the conflict between David and Nabal not only saves her household from destruction but also earns her the respect and admiration of those around her. Through Abigail's story, readers are reminded of the importance of seeking peace, practicing discernment, and trusting in God's providence, even in the midst of life's most difficult challenges.

Delilah

Delilah, a significant but controversial figure in the biblical narrative, is best known for her role in the story of Samson, found in the book of Judges. Her story unfolds in Judges chapters 16, where she is depicted as a woman of deceit who betrays Samson, the Israelite judge, and strongman. Delilah's character and actions raise complex questions about power, betrayal, and the consequences of manipulation, making her a compelling yet enigmatic figure in the biblical narrative.

Delilah's introduction in Judges 16 portrays her as a woman of Philistine descent, living in the valley of Sorek. Despite her background, Delilah forms a relationship with Samson, who becomes infatuated with her. The Philistine rulers, seeking to capture and subdue Samson, approach Delilah and offer her a substantial sum of money in exchange for discovering the source of his strength.

Delilah's role in the story becomes apparent as she repeatedly attempts to uncover the secret of Samson's strength. Through a series of manipulative tactics and deceitful questioning, Delilah gradually wears down Samson's resistance and persuades him to reveal the source of his strength: his uncut hair, which symbolizes his consecration to God as a Nazirite.

Upon learning Samson's secret, Delilah betrays him to the Philistine rulers, who seize him, blind him, and imprison him. The consequences of Delilah's betrayal are severe, leading to Samson's downfall and eventual death. However, Delilah's ultimate fate is left ambiguous in the biblical narrative, leaving readers to speculate about her motives and intentions.

Delilah's story raises complex moral and ethical questions about the nature of power, manipulation, and betrayal. While she is often portrayed as a villainous figure who exploits Samson for personal gain, some interpretations suggest that Delilah may have acted out of desperation or coercion, seeking to secure her own safety or advance her position in a patriarchal society.

Despite the ambiguity surrounding her character, Delilah's story serves as a cautionary tale about the dangers of deception and the consequences of betraying trust. Her actions highlight the destructive power of manipulation and the importance of discernment in relationships. Moreover, Delilah's story underscores the vulnerability of even the strongest individuals to the influence of others and the importance of guarding one's heart and boundaries.

Delilah's story in the Bible is one of intrigue, betrayal, and moral complexity. While her character raises challenging questions about motives and intentions, her role in the story of Samson serves as a cautionary tale about the dangers of manipulation and the consequences of betrayal.

Through Delilah's story, readers are reminded of the importance of integrity, discernment, and trustworthiness in relationships, as well as the need to guard against the lure of power and deceit.

Jezebel

Jezebel, a figure notorious in the Old Testament, is remembered for her influential and controversial role as queen of Israel during the reign of King Ahab. Her story, found primarily in the books of 1 and 2 Kings, offers profound insights into themes of power, manipulation, and the consequences of idolatry. Despite being reviled as a symbol of wickedness and tyranny, Jezebel's story prompts reflection on the dangers of unchecked ambition and the perversion of spiritual values.

Jezebel's introduction in the biblical narrative occurs when she marries Ahab, the king of Israel, as part of a political alliance between Israel and the kingdom of Sidon. From the outset, Jezebel is portrayed as a woman of fierce determination and unwavering devotion to the worship of Baal, the pagan god of the Sidonians. Her influence over Ahab leads him to abandon the worship of Yahweh, the God of Israel, and embrace the practices of idolatry and paganism.

One of the most infamous incidents involving Jezebel occurs in 1 Kings 21, where she orchestrates the murder of Naboth, a righteous man who refuses to sell his vineyard to Ahab. Through deception and manipulation, Jezebel arranges for Naboth to be falsely accused of blasphemy and stoned to death, allowing Ahab to seize the vineyard for himself. This act of injustice and cruelty underscores Jezebel's ruthless pursuit of power and her willingness to sacrifice innocent lives to achieve her goals.

Jezebel's influence over Ahab extends beyond matters of politics and governance to matters of faith and spirituality. She actively promotes the worship of Baal and encourages the persecution of prophets and followers of Yahweh, leading to a spiritual crisis in Israel and a conflict between the prophets of God and the prophets of Baal on Mount Carmel.

Despite her formidable reputation as a queen and a prophetess of Baal, Jezebel's story ultimately ends in ignominy and tragedy. In 2 Kings 9, Jehu, a commander in the army of Israel, is anointed king by the prophet Elisha and commissioned to execute God's judgment on the house of Ahab. Jehu confronts Jezebel in Jezreel and orders her servants to throw her out of a window, leading to her death and subsequent consumption by dogs, fulfilling the prophecy of Elijah.

Jezebel's narrative unfolds as a stark cautionary tale, illustrating the perilous consequences of unbridled ambition and the distortion of spiritual principles. Her relentless quest for dominion, coupled with a willingness to compromise morality and forsake justice in pursuit of self-interest, stands as a stark admonition to leaders and individuals alike regarding the insidious allure of pride and idolatry, ultimately corroding the fabric of ethical leadership and spiritual integrity.

Jezebel's story in the Bible is a sobering reminder of the dangers of unchecked ambition and the perversion of spiritual values. Her ruthless pursuit of power and her manipulation of religious beliefs led to tragedy and destruction, serving as a cautionary tale for leaders and individuals about the consequences of forsaking righteousness and embracing wickedness. Through Jezebel's story, readers are prompted to reflect on the importance of integrity, humility, and obedience to God's commands in the pursuit of true greatness and lasting significance.

Hannah

Hannah, a figure of faith and perseverance, is celebrated in the Old Testament for her poignant story of prayer, longing, and divine intervention. Her narrative, found in the book of 1 Samuel, offers profound insights into themes of faith, motherhood, and the sovereignty of God. Despite facing adversity and heartache, Hannah's unwavering trust in God's promises leads to a miraculous blessing and the birth of her son, Samuel, who becomes one of the greatest prophets in Israel's history.

Hannah's story begins in the town of Ramathaim-Zophim, where she is introduced as one of two wives of Elkanah, a devout man who regularly makes offerings to the Lord. Despite Elkanah's love and devotion, Hannah experiences deep sorrow and anguish due to her inability to conceive a child. In a culture where a woman's worth and identity were often tied to her ability to bear children, Hannah's barrenness is a source of profound shame and grief.

Year after year, Hannah accompanies Elkanah to the tabernacle at Shiloh to make sacrifices to the Lord. On one such occasion, as Hannah pours out her heart in prayer, she makes a vow to God, promising that if He grants her a son, she will dedicate him to the Lord's service for his entire life. In a moment of deep spiritual surrender, Hannah entrusts her deepest longing and desire to God, demonstrating her faith and humility.

God hears Hannah's prayer and responds with compassion and grace. In due time, Hannah conceives and gives birth to a son, whom she names Samuel, meaning "heard by God." In a beautiful expression of gratitude and praise, Hannah offers a heartfelt prayer of thanksgiving, known as the "Song of Hannah," in which she extols God's faithfulness and sovereignty and rejoices in His provision and blessing.

Hannah's story is a powerful testament to the transformative power of prayer and faith. Her willingness to surrender her deepest desires to God and trust in His timing and providence serves as a model of spiritual resilience and steadfastness. Through Hannah's example, readers are encouraged to bring their hopes, fears, and longings before God in prayer, knowing that He hears and answers according to His will.

Moreover, Hannah's story underscores the importance of keeping one's commitments to God. Despite the natural maternal instinct to cling to her son, Hannah remains true to her vow and fulfills her promise to dedicate Samuel to the Lord's service. Her sacrificial obedience sets the stage for Samuel's remarkable life and ministry as a prophet, judge, and spiritual leader in Israel.

Hannah's narrative in the Bible stands as an enduring testament to the profound impact of faith, prayer, and unwavering obedience. Her transformative journey from the depths of barrenness and sorrow to the heights of motherhood and joy serves as an uplifting source of inspiration for believers across generations. Through Hannah's poignant tale, readers are vividly reminded of God's unfailing faithfulness, His remarkable capacity to transform mourning into rejoicing, and His gracious inclination to attentively hear and answer the fervent prayers of His faithful people.

Deborah

Deborah, a prophetess and judge in ancient Israel, stands as a powerful symbol of courage, wisdom, and leadership in the Old Testament. Her story, found in the book of Judges, offers profound insights into themes of faith, justice, and the empowerment of women. Despite living in a male-dominated society, Deborah's remarkable character and God-given abilities enable her to rise to prominence and play a pivotal role in the deliverance of Israel from oppression.

Deborah's story unfolds during a turbulent period in Israel's history, characterized by cycles of apostasy, oppression, and deliverance. As a prophetess, Deborah serves as a mouthpiece for God, delivering messages of guidance and warning to the people of Israel. Her wisdom and discernment earn her the respect and admiration of both men and women, establishing her as a trusted leader and counselor in the nation.

One of the most significant events in Deborah's story occurs when she summons Barak, a military commander, and instructs him to lead an army against the oppressive Canaanite king Jabin and his general Sisera. Despite Barak's initial hesitation, Deborah assures him of God's presence and victory, declaring, "The Lord will sell Sisera into the hand of a woman" (Judges 4:9). Deborah's prophetic insight and unwavering faith inspire Barak to mobilize the Israelite army and confront their enemies.

Under Deborah's leadership and guidance, the Israelites achieve a decisive victory over the Canaanite forces at the Battle of Mount Tabor. God intervenes supernaturally, causing confusion and panic among the enemy ranks and enabling the Israelites to overcome their adversaries. The defeat of Sisera and his army marks a significant turning point in Israel's history, leading to a period of peace and prosperity under Deborah's leadership.

In addition to her role as a military leader, Deborah also serves as a judge and arbiter of disputes among the people of Israel. She holds court under a palm tree in the hill country of Ephraim, where she dispenses justice and settles disputes according to God's laws and principles. Deborah's commitment to righteousness and fairness earns her the respect and admiration of the Israelites, who recognize her as a wise and just ruler.

Deborah's story challenges conventional notions of gender roles and highlights the importance of women's leadership and empowerment in the service of God's kingdom. Despite living in a patriarchal society, Deborah's remarkable character and God-given abilities enable her to break through cultural barriers and fulfill her calling as a prophetess, judge, and military leader. Her story serves as a powerful reminder of the value and importance of women's contributions to the work of God and His kingdom.

Deborah's narrative in the Bible blazes with the electrifying power of faith, courage, and visionary leadership. Her resolute dedication to God's divine agenda and her fearless response to His call stand as a beacon of inspiration and empowerment for believers of every era. Through Deborah's captivating tale, readers are invigorated by the profound revelation of God's transformative presence and unparalleled might in the lives of His people. Her story ignites the realization that individuals—irrespective of gender or origin—possess the boundless potential to leave an indelible mark on the world, all to magnify His glorious name.

Huldah

Huldah, a lesser-known but significant figure in the Old Testament, is recognized for her role as a prophetess during the reign of King Josiah of Judah. Despite being overshadowed by other prophets such as Isaiah and Jeremiah, Huldah's story offers valuable insights into themes of faithfulness, discernment, and the authority of

God's word. Her narrative, found in 2 Kings 22 and 2 Chronicles 34, highlights the importance of seeking and heeding divine guidance in times of spiritual crisis and renewal.

Huldah's story unfolds against the backdrop of a tumultuous period in Judah's history, marked by idolatry, corruption, and social injustice. King Josiah, who ascends to the throne at a young age, seeks to reform the nation and restore worship of the one true God. In the eighteenth year of his reign, Josiah orders the renovation of the temple in Jerusalem, during which the Book of the Law is discovered.

Upon hearing the words of the Law read aloud, Josiah is deeply troubled by the nation's disobedience and disregard for God's commands. Recognizing the gravity of the situation, Josiah sends a delegation, including the high priest Hilkiah, to consult with Huldah, a trusted prophetess known for her wisdom and insight.

Huldah's response to the delegation's inquiry is both authoritative and prophetic. She affirms the divine origin of the message contained in the Book of the Law and delivers a message of judgment and restoration to the king and the people of Judah. Despite the nation's sins and idolatry, Huldah assures Josiah that God has seen his humility and repentance and will spare him from witnessing the calamity that will befall Judah.

Huldah's pivotal role as a prophetess and her authoritative proclamation of God's word emphasize the critical significance of seeking divine guidance and wholeheartedly obeying His commands. Her prophetic message acts as a catalyst for Josiah's sweeping reforms and the subsequent spiritual reawakening of the nation. Under Josiah's visionary leadership, the people of Judah experience a profound season of repentance and revival, culminating in the restoration of authentic worship and the decisive eradication of idolatry from their midst.

Despite her relatively brief appearance in the biblical narrative, Huldah's story serves as a reminder of the vital role played by women in the work of God's kingdom. Her example challenges traditional notions of gender roles and highlights the importance of women's voices and contributions in matters of faith and leadership.

Huldah's story in the Bible is a testament to the power of faithfulness, discernment, and obedience to God's word. Her role as a prophetess and her authoritative interpretation of divine revelation serve as an inspiration and encouragement to believers of all generations. Through Huldah's story, readers are reminded of the importance of seeking divine guidance and heeding the voice of God in times of spiritual crisis and renewal.

Queen Esther

Queen Esther, a prominent figure in the Old Testament, is celebrated for her bravery, wisdom, and faithfulness in the face of adversity. Her story, chronicled in the book of Esther, offers profound insights into themes of courage, providence, and the triumph of righteousness over evil. Despite living in a time of peril and uncertainty, Esther's unwavering trust in God and her willingness to risk her life for the sake of her people exemplify the transformative power of faith and obedience.

Esther's story begins in the Persian Empire during the reign of King Xerxes, also known as Ahasuerus. As an orphaned Israelite girl raised by her cousin Mordecai, Esther finds herself thrust into a position of unexpected influence when she is selected to be part of the king's harem. Despite her humble origins and precarious circumstances, Esther's beauty and grace captivate the king, ultimately leading to her selection as queen.

Esther's rise to power coincides with a plot orchestrated by the king's chief advisor, Haman, to annihilate the Israelite people throughout the empire. Unaware of her Israelite heritage, Esther initially hesitates to intervene, fearing for her own safety. However, Mordecai urges her to use her position of influence to intercede on behalf of her people, declaring, "Who knows whether you have not come to the kingdom for such a time as this?" (Esther 4:14).

Inspired by Mordecai's words and guided by her faith in God, Esther resolves to take action. She risks her life by approaching the king uninvited, a violation of royal protocol, to plead for the salvation of her people. In a dramatic turn of events, Esther reveals her Israelite identity to the king and exposes Haman's nefarious plot to destroy the Hebrews.

Through a series of providential interventions orchestrated by God, Esther's courage and wisdom ultimately lead to the defeat of Haman and the salvation of the Israelite people. The king rescinds his decree, allowing the Hebrews to defend themselves against their enemies, resulting in a decisive victory and the establishment of the festival of Purim to commemorate their deliverance.

Esther's narrative stands as an enduring monument to the formidable forces of faith, courage, and unwavering obedience amidst daunting adversity. Her extraordinary readiness to stake everything on behalf of her people epitomizes the profound influence of righteous deeds on the grand stage of human events, magnifying the divine providence woven into every strand of life. Through Esther's resolute example, readers are invigorated to embrace trust in God's steadfast faithfulness and to embody willing vessels for His sovereign plans, even amid the most formidable trials.

Esther's story in the Bible is a powerful reminder of the triumph of righteousness over evil and the transformative power of faith and obedience. Her bravery, wisdom, and faithfulness continue to inspire believers of all generations to stand firm in their convictions and to trust in God's providence, knowing that He is able to work all things together for the good of those who love Him.

Elizabeth

Elizabeth, a figure of faith and resilience in the New Testament, is best known as the mother of John the Baptist. Her story, found in the Gospel of Luke, offers profound insights into themes of faith, redemption, and the fulfillment of God's promises. Despite facing years of barrenness and societal stigma, Elizabeth's unwavering trust in God's faithfulness ultimately leads to the miraculous conception and birth of her son, John, who plays a pivotal role in preparing the way for the Messiah.

Elizabeth's story begins with her husband, Zechariah, serving as a priest in the temple. Despite their devoutness and righteousness before God, Elizabeth and Zechariah are childless, a source of great sorrow and shame in ancient Hebrew culture. However, their barrenness does not diminish their faithfulness to God, as they continue to serve Him faithfully and observe His commandments.

In a moment of divine intervention, the angel Gabriel appears to Zechariah while he is serving in the temple, announcing that Elizabeth will conceive and bear a son who will be named John. Initially incredulous due to their old age, Zechariah questions the angel's message and is struck mute until the birth of his son. Meanwhile, Elizabeth receives the news with faith and humility, rejoicing in God's mercy and provision.

Elizabeth's pregnancy becomes a source of great joy and blessing, as she testifies to God's faithfulness and goodness to her family and community. When Mary, the mother of Jesus, visits Elizabeth during her own miraculous pregnancy,

Elizabeth is filled with the Holy Spirit and prophesies the greatness of the child in Mary's womb, recognizing Jesus as the long-awaited Messiah.

The birth of John the Baptist fulfills God's promises to Elizabeth and Zechariah, bringing joy and celebration to their household and community. John grows up to become a powerful prophet and forerunner of Jesus, fulfilling the prophecy of Isaiah to prepare the way for the Lord and proclaim the coming of the Kingdom of God.

Elizabeth's narrative serves as a profound illustration of the transformative potency of faith and obedience amid challenging circumstances. Despite enduring years of barrenness and disappointment, Elizabeth steadfastly upholds her faith in God and His promises, demonstrating unwavering trust in His perfect timing and provision. Her exemplary conduct inspires believers to persist in their faith journeys, fortified by the assurance of God's unwavering faithfulness and His ability to exceed human expectations with His boundless accomplishments.

Elizabeth's story in the Bible stands as a resounding testament to the enduring faithfulness and provision of God for those who wholeheartedly rely on Him. Her unwavering commitment and resilience in the face of adversity serve as an enduring source of inspiration for believers across epochs, imparting the vital lesson of persevering in faith and obedience. Through Elizabeth's narrative, believers are encouraged to entrust themselves to God's steadfast promises, confident that He is faithful to fulfill His divine purposes in their lives, surpassing all conceivable expectations.

Mary (Mother of Jesus)

Mary, the mother of Jesus, occupies a central and revered role in both Biblical theology and devotion. Her story, as depicted in the Gospels of Matthew, Mark, Luke, and John, is characterized by themes of faith, humility, and obedience, making her a symbol of divine grace and maternal love. Mary's extraordinary journey from an ordinary Hebrew girl to the mother of the Savior of humanity offers profound insights into the human experience and the divine plan of redemption.

Mary's story begins in the small Galilean village of Nazareth, where she is introduced as a young virgin engaged to a man named Joseph, a descendant of King David. In a moment of divine visitation, the angel Gabriel appears to Mary, announcing that she has been chosen by God to conceive and bear a son who will be named Jesus. Despite her initial confusion and fear, Mary responds with humility and faith, declaring, "Behold, I am the servant of the Lord; let it be to me according to your word" (Luke 1:38).

Mary's willingness to submit to God's will and participate in His redemptive plan exemplifies her profound faith and trust in God's promises. Despite the social stigma and personal risks associated with her miraculous pregnancy, Mary embraces her role as the mother of the Messiah with courage and conviction, knowing that she has been chosen for a divine purpose.

Throughout her life, Mary remains a steadfast witness to the miraculous nature of Jesus' birth and ministry. She experiences the joy of seeing her son grow and develop, marveling at His wisdom and understanding. Mary accompanies Jesus during His ministry, offering support and encouragement, and is present at significant moments in His life, including His crucifixion and resurrection.

Mary's role as the mother of Jesus is characterized by both profound joy and deep sorrow. While she experiences the privilege of nurturing and caring for the Son of God, she also endures the anguish of witnessing His suffering and death on the cross. Despite her grief, Mary remains faithful to God's plan, trusting in His promises of redemption and resurrection.

Mary's significance extends beyond her role as the mother of Jesus to become a symbol of maternal love and compassion for all humanity. Her example of faith, humility, and obedience inspires believers of all generations to emulate her virtues and entrust themselves to the providence of God.

Mary Magdalene

Mary Magdalene, a prominent figure in the New Testament, is often portrayed as a symbol of devotion, redemption, and witness to the resurrection of Jesus Christ. Her story, recorded in the Gospels of Matthew, Mark, Luke, and John, offers profound insights into themes of forgiveness, faith, and the transformative power of encountering the risen Lord. Despite being misunderstood and marginalized in some historical interpretations, Mary Magdalene's role as a faithful disciple and witness to the resurrection serves as a testament to the inclusive and transformative nature of Jesus' ministry.

Mary Magdalene is introduced in the Gospels as a woman from the town of Magdala in Galilee, who becomes one of Jesus' most devoted followers. She is depicted as a woman who has experienced great healing and deliverance from evil spirits through Jesus' ministry, leading her to become a faithful supporter of His mission. Alongside other women, Mary Magdalene accompanies Jesus and the disciples on their journeys, ministering to their needs and providing support out of her own resources.

One of the most significant moments in Mary Magdalene's story occurs at the crucifixion of Jesus, where she stands faithfully at the foot of the cross, witnessing His suffering and death. Despite the trauma and despair of seeing her beloved teacher and friend crucified, Mary Magdalene remains steadfast in her devotion, unwilling to abandon Jesus in His hour of need.

Mary Magdalene's most profound encounter with Jesus comes on the morning of the resurrection, when she visits the tomb and discovers that it is empty. In a moment of profound confusion and grief, Mary Magdalene encounters the risen Lord, who appears to her in the garden outside the tomb. At first, she mistakes Jesus for the gardener, but when He calls her by name, she recognizes Him and responds with overwhelming joy and reverence.

Jesus entrusts Mary Magdalene with the sacred task of bearing witness to His resurrection, instructing her to go and tell the disciples the good news. Mary Magdalene becomes the first to proclaim the resurrection, earning her the title of "apostle to the apostles" in Christian tradition. Her faithful testimony to the resurrection serves as the foundation of Christian faith and hope, inspiring believers throughout history to proclaim the risen Christ.

Despite her central role in the resurrection narrative, Mary Magdalene has often been misunderstood and misrepresented in Christian tradition. In some accounts, she has been conflated with other biblical figures, such as the unnamed woman who anoints Jesus' feet or the repentant sinner who washes His feet with her tears. However, modern scholarship has sought to restore Mary Magdalene's rightful place as a faithful disciple and witness to the resurrection.

Mary Magdalene's narrative in the Bible resonates as a profound testament to the life-altering impact of encountering the risen Lord. Her remarkable odyssey—from a woman profoundly healed and liberated by Jesus to an unwavering disciple and primary witness of the resurrection—stands as a vivid illustration of unwavering devotion, profound faith, and unyielding courage. Mary Magdalene's pivotal role in the resurrection chronicle challenges traditional constructs of gender and societal status, affirming the inclusive and transformative essence of Jesus' ministry. Through her steadfast witness, Mary Magdalene beckons believers to embrace a personal encounter with the risen Christ and to fervently proclaim the life-changing news of His resurrection to the world.

Martha

Martha, the sister of Lazarus, is a notable figure in the New Testament, depicted as a woman of faith, service, and devotion to Jesus Christ. Her story, found primarily in the Gospel of John, offers profound insights into themes of discipleship, faith, and the importance of prioritizing spiritual matters over temporal concerns. Despite her occasional moments of doubt and frustration, Martha's unwavering commitment to Jesus and her willingness to serve Him exemplify the transformative power of faith and discipleship.

Martha is introduced in the Gospel of John as one of the sisters of Lazarus, whom Jesus raises from the dead in one of His most famous miracles. Along with her sister Mary, Martha welcomes Jesus into their home in the village of Bethany and extends hospitality to Him and His disciples. From the outset, Martha's character is defined by her active service and practicality, as she busies herself with the tasks of preparing food and ensuring the comfort of her guests.

One of the most well-known episodes involving Martha occurs in Luke's Gospel, where she becomes frustrated with her sister Mary for sitting at Jesus' feet and listening to His teaching while she is left to serve alone. In her frustration, Martha appeals to Jesus, saying, "Lord, do you not care that my sister has left me to serve alone? Tell her then to help me" (Luke 10:40). Jesus responds gently but firmly, commending Mary for choosing the "good portion," which will not be taken away from her.

This incident serves as a valuable lesson in discipleship and priorities. While Martha's concern for hospitality and service is commendable, Jesus gently redirects her focus to the importance of spiritual nourishment and relationship with God. Martha's initial frustration highlights the tension between action and contemplation, service and devotion, that many believers wrestle with in their own lives.

Despite her momentary lapse in understanding, Martha's faith in Jesus remains steadfast throughout His ministry. When her brother Lazarus falls ill and dies, Martha expresses her confidence in Jesus' power to heal and even to raise the dead. Her statement, "Lord, if you had been here, my brother would not have died. But even now I know that whatever you ask from God, God will give you" (John 11:21-22), reflects her unwavering trust in Jesus' authority and divine identity.

Jesus' subsequent raising of Lazarus from the dead serves as a dramatic demonstration of His power over death and the fulfillment of Martha's faith. In this pivotal moment, Martha's belief in Jesus as the resurrection and the life is confirmed, and her witness to this miraculous event strengthens the faith of those around her.

Martha is a compelling example of faith, service, and devotion in the New Testament. Despite her occasional moments of doubt and frustration, Martha's unwavering commitment to Jesus and her willingness to serve Him exemplify the transformative power of faith and discipleship. Through her story, readers are challenged to prioritize spiritual matters over temporal concerns and to cultivate a deeper relationship with God through contemplation, prayer, and service. Martha's example serves as an inspiration to believers of all generations, reminding them of the importance of placing their trust in Jesus as the resurrection and the life, who has power over death and offers eternal life to all who believe in Him.

Mary of Bethany

Mary of Bethany, a beloved figure in the New Testament, is celebrated for her profound love, devotion, and intimacy with Jesus Christ. Her story, found in the Gospels of Luke, John, and Matthew, offers profound insights into themes of discipleship, worship, and the transformative power of encountering the presence of God. Despite her relatively brief appearances in the biblical narrative, Mary's actions and words leave an indelible mark, revealing her deep understanding of Jesus' identity and mission.

Mary is introduced in the Gospel of Luke as the sister of Martha and Lazarus, who reside in the village of Bethany. In the Gospel of John, Mary is depicted as the woman who anoints Jesus' feet with expensive perfume and wipes them with her hair, an act of extravagant worship and devotion. This poignant scene captures the essence of Mary's character—a woman whose love for Jesus knows no bounds and who expresses her devotion in a deeply personal and sacrificial manner.

One of the most memorable episodes involving Mary occurs in the Gospel of Luke, where she is depicted as sitting at Jesus' feet and listening to His teaching while her sister Martha is busy with preparations. When Martha complains to Jesus about her sister's lack of assistance, Jesus responds by affirming Mary's choice, saying, "Martha, Martha, you are anxious and troubled about many things, but one thing is necessary. Mary has chosen the good portion, which will not be taken away from her" (Luke 10:41-42).

This scene illustrates Mary's deep spiritual insight and her recognition of the importance of prioritizing relationship with Jesus above all else. While Martha is preoccupied with serving and hospitality, Mary understands the significance of sitting at Jesus' feet and listening to His words, recognizing that true fulfillment and satisfaction are found in communion with Him.

Another significant episode involving Mary occurs in the Gospel of John, where she anoints Jesus' feet with costly perfume in preparation for His burial. This act of extravagant love and devotion is met with criticism from some of the disciples, who question the wastefulness of Mary's gesture. However, Jesus defends Mary's actions, commending her for her foresight and recognizing the significance of her act as a preparation for His impending death and burial.

Through her actions and words, Mary of Bethany exemplifies the essence of true discipleship—a life marked by love, devotion, and intimacy with Jesus Christ. Her willingness to prioritize relationship with Jesus above all else serves as a model for believers of all generations, challenging them to cultivate a deeper and more intimate walk with God.

Mary of Bethany is a beloved figure in the New Testament, celebrated for her profound love, devotion, and intimacy with Jesus Christ. Through her actions and words, Mary exemplifies the essence of true discipleship—a life marked by love, devotion, and intimacy with Jesus Christ. Her willingness to prioritize relationship with Jesus above all else serves as a model for believers of all generations, challenging them to cultivate a deeper and more intimate walk with God. Mary's story continues to inspire and encourage believers today, reminding them of the transformative power of encountering the presence of God and the profound impact of a life lived in devotion to Him.

Samaritan Woman

The Samaritan Woman at the Well, a significant figure in the New Testament, is celebrated for her encounter with Jesus Christ, which led to her transformation and the spread of the Gospel in her community. Her story, found in the Gospel of John, offers profound insights into themes of identity, inclusion, and the transformative power of encountering Jesus. Despite her marginalized status as a Samaritan woman, the encounter at the well reveals her thirst for truth and her openness to the message of salvation.

The Samaritan Woman's encounter with Jesus takes place at Jacob's well, a location of historical and spiritual significance. Jesus, weary from His journey, asks the woman for a drink of water, initiating a conversation that transcends cultural barriers and societal norms. In response, the Samaritan Woman expresses surprise that an Israelite man would speak to a Samaritan woman, highlighting the deep-seated animosity and division between the two ethnic groups.

As the conversation progresses, Jesus reveals His true identity as the Messiah, offering the Samaritan Woman "living water" that will satisfy her spiritual thirst and lead to eternal life. Intrigued by Jesus' words, the woman engages Him in theological dialogue, expressing her desire for this "living water" and acknowledging her need for spiritual nourishment.

Throughout their conversation, Jesus demonstrates His knowledge of the Samaritan Woman's personal history, including her marital status and past relationships. Rather than condemning her for her past sins and indiscretions, Jesus offers her grace and forgiveness, inviting her to embrace a new identity as a child of God.

In response to Jesus' revelation, the Samaritan Woman's heart is stirred, and she recognizes Jesus as the Messiah, proclaiming, "Sir, I perceive that you are a prophet" (John 4:19). Filled with newfound faith and zeal, she leaves her water jar behind and rushes back to her village to share her encounter with Jesus, inviting others to come and meet Him for themselves.

The Samaritan Woman's bold witness leads to the conversion of many in her village, who come to believe in Jesus as the Savior of the world. Through her testimony, she becomes a channel of God's grace and a herald of the Gospel, demonstrating the transformative power of encountering Jesus and embracing His message of salvation.

The Samaritan Woman at the Well stands as a compelling testament to profound spiritual hunger and a remarkable openness to God's truth, transcending societal status or ethnic origin. Her transformative encounter with Jesus vividly underscores the expansive inclusivity of God's kingdom and His unwavering desire to extend salvation to all earnest seekers of truth and faith.

The Samaritan Woman at the Well is a significant figure in the New Testament, celebrated for her encounter with Jesus Christ, which led to her transformation and the spread of the Gospel in her community. Her story serves as a powerful reminder of the transformative power of encountering Jesus and embracing His message of salvation. Through her bold witness and testimony, she becomes a channel of God's grace and a herald of the Gospel, demonstrating the inclusivity of God's kingdom and His desire to offer salvation to all who seek Him in faith.

Joannna

Joanna, though her appearances in the Bible are relatively brief, is a figure of significance, particularly in the Gospel accounts of Jesus' life and ministry. Her story, while sparse in detail, provides glimpses into the diverse group of individuals who were drawn to Jesus and the impact of His teachings on their lives. Joanna's dedication, generosity, and faithfulness exemplify the transformative power of encountering Jesus and the profound influence He had on those who followed Him.

Joanna is first mentioned in the Gospel of Luke, where she is described as the wife of Chuza, who served as the steward or manager of Herod's household. This detail alone suggests that Joanna came from a relatively affluent or influential background, as Herod's household was associated with wealth and power. Despite her privileged position, Joanna is drawn to Jesus and becomes one of His followers, indicating her willingness to break social norms and align herself with a movement that challenged the status quo.

In Luke 8:1-3, Joanna is listed among the women who accompanied Jesus and the twelve disciples, providing for them out of her own resources. This act of generosity and support demonstrates Joanna's commitment to Jesus' ministry and her willingness to use her resources to advance His kingdom. Her inclusion in this group of women suggests that she played an active role in Jesus' inner circle and was valued for her contributions to His mission.

Another significant mention of Joanna occurs in the Gospel of Luke's account of the resurrection. After Jesus' crucifixion, Joanna is one of the women who goes to the tomb to anoint His body with spices. To their amazement, they find the tomb empty and encounter angels who proclaim Jesus' resurrection. Joanna and the other women rush to tell the disciples the good news, but their testimony is initially met with disbelief. Nevertheless, their faithful witness lays the foundation for the spread of the Gospel and the proclamation of Jesus' resurrection to the ends of the earth.

While Joanna's story may be brief, her dedication, generosity, and faithfulness serve as an inspiration to believers throughout the ages. Despite the challenges and risks associated with following Jesus, Joanna remained steadfast in her commitment to Him and His teachings. Her willingness to use her resources for the advancement of God's kingdom and her faithful witness to the resurrection underscore the transformative power of encountering Jesus and the profound impact He had on the lives of those who followed Him.

Joanna emerges as a notable figure in the New Testament, particularly highlighted in the Gospel narratives depicting Jesus' life and ministry. Though her story is brief, it offers profound glimpses into the diverse array of individuals drawn to Jesus and the profound impact of His teachings on their lives. Joanna's unwavering dedication, remarkable generosity, and steadfast faithfulness vividly exemplify the transformative influence of encountering Jesus and the profound imprint He left on those who chose to follow Him. Her narrative stands as a poignant reminder of the enduring value of sacrificial service, steadfast witness, and unyielding commitment to the cause of Christ.

About the Author

Karajah Yashar is an accomplished author and entrepreneur with a deep-rooted passion for biblical scholarship. A graduate of Rutgers University, Karajah has worked professionally for both Rutgers and the University of Central Florida.

Karajah Yashar is best known as the founder and CEO of Blackstone Publishing, a reputable Orlando-based company specializing in scholarly works focused on biblical themes. Under his leadership, Blackstone Publishing has become a recognized name in the realm of biblical literature, offering insightful and thought-provoking publications.

This project reflects Karajah's personal convictions and family values, as he draws inspiration from the strong women in his own life. He firmly believes in the significant role women play in God's kingdom and seeks to illuminate their stories and contributions through his scholarly writings.

"Favour is deceitful, and beauty is vain: but a woman that feareth the LORD, she shall be praised."

Proverbs 31:30

www.ingramcontent.com/pod-product-compliance
Lightning Source LLC
Chambersburg PA
CBHW081755120626
46587CB00033B/351